MW01171366

"The Mouse in the Manger"

Written by Jersey Doll

Illustrated by DooDad

This book is dedicated to:

My Lord God, for only through Him
has all this been made possible.

My parents and grandparents, all of them,
for their lifelong support and inspiration.

For Isaac, my dear brother,
whom I love so very much.

To my beloved Slykat, who has been with me
every step of the way and offered limitless
inspiration and support. I love you.

Table of Contents

Preface

I fell in love with reading, writing and performing music at a young age. As soon as I could read, I began writing stories. One day, I excitedly told my mother, "I want to write something that everyone will remember!" And she looked at me, smiled and said, "So, do that."

As the years have passed, and I have spent the majority of them teaching music and performance, I have experienced so much joy from watching children learn how to work together as a team to perform and become artists themselves. I have witnessed children gain their self confidence through acting and speaking on stage. This story was born in a little classroom, where I told it to my students while twisting up little balloon mice for each of them to have. Today, I am sharing it with all of you. This story is very close to my heart and shows how even a small act of kindness and compassion can make a big difference in the world. Love and peace.

Introduction

I wanted this story to come to life for both the children who might read it and those who read it to them. I have always loved stories that I could feel I was a part of, and I included for you teachers and parents, some ideas at the end of this book to make that happen. There are also activity pages and suggestions for having children act out the story on stage. My goal was to incorporate values and virtues into this story as well.

You will find that Matthew the Mouse, our main character, experiences and overcomes fear, works hard, shows compassion, possesses a helpful spirit, and even as a small animal, communicates with his Creator. While traditionally, the birth of Jesus is usually celebrated during the Christmas season, this story may be enjoyed at any time of the year. Enjoy!

"Crash--Boom--Bang!" What was that noise? Matthew rubbed the sleep out of his eyes and ran to see what was happening. There were people in his house, and this was very strange.

Matthew was a field mouse and his house was a stable, which sat behind an inn, a place where people slept and ate food. People stayed inside and animals lived outside, in the stable. What were they doing there? People came in and out only to feed and water their animals. There was no room for this man and woman, because the inn was full, and they had traveled a long way to get here, to the city of Bethlehem.

Matthew had a busy night ahead, so he went back to sleep. Field mice are nocturnal, which means they stay awake at night. That is when they work on building their house and finding food for their family. It is very important that they hide from larger and more dangerous animals that may think a mouse might be good to eat. Matthew was always careful and quiet as he went about his work.

As it became night, Matthew was woken up AGAIN by loud noises. This time, by an even stranger sound. What could it be this time? Matthew went to see where the noise was coming from. It was coming from the manger, where they fed the donkeys, horses and other animals hay and grain. The noise kept getting louder.

As Matthew got closer, climbed up the side of the manger and looked in, he was surprised to see, of all things, a BABY! A baby had been born right in his house and was using the manger as a bed! His mother called him, "Jesus", because the Lord God had told her to.

It was beginning to get dark and cold outside. Matthew thought about his own family and how hard he worked to keep his children warm and safe. There was not much to keep the Baby warm in the manger and Matthew wondered about this. He prepared for the busy night and set off.

Matthew looked for food in the inn first. He would find scraps of bread, fruit, cheese, vegetables and things that he and his family could eat.

He would carry as much as he could, careful not to be seen by the people. They didn't like when a mouse was in THEIR house, so he had to move fast and stay out of sight.

As Matthew brought the last of what he found home, he went to check on the Baby, sleeping in the manger. Brrr....it was getting colder. As he scurried into the stable, there was a Light so bright, it hurt his little mouse eyes. He squinted to see what It was. Where was It coming from? It wasn't a fire, or a lantern. It wasn't a candle, but It lighted up the whole place as bright as the Sun!

He went outside and saw a giant Star, big and bright. It was the biggest he had ever seen in his life and It was shining right over the stable!

People were coming and running towards the stable, so Matthew hid to see what was happening. As they came closer, he saw that they were shepherds who had come all the way from the fields to see this Baby! Matthew knew THIS Baby must be very special, so he listened to the story the shepherds told when they got there. As the shepherds were watching their flocks of sheep and getting ready to sleep, an angel came to them from the Lord and a bright Light shone down from Heaven that scared them. The angel had a special message and this is what they said,

"Fear not: for behold, I bring you good tidings of great joy, which shall be to all people. For unto you is born this day in the city of David a Saviour, which is Christ the Lord. And this shall be a sign unto you; Ye shall find the babe wrapped in swaddling clothes, lying in a manger. " Luke 2:10-12 KJV

Matthew heard the shepherds say that right after the angel told them this, t h e r e   w e r e   o t h e r   a n g e l s EVERYWHERE, singing and praising God saying, "Glory to God in the highest, and on earth peace, good will toward men." Luke 2:14 KJV When the angels left, the shepherds ran to Bethlehem, the city of David, to go look for the special Baby. They found Him there in the manger, just like the angel said.

When they came to the stable, they were so happy. Everyone was excited, and after worshipping the Baby Jesus, the shepherds ran to go tell everyone they knew. Matthew knew this Baby must be the most special Baby in the world ever to be born and he wanted to help in some way.

He thought and thought about what he could do and began gathering straw in his mouth and carrying it to the manger, to fill in spaces where the cold night air might get in. He worked for the rest of the night to bring straw to keep the Baby Jesus warm.

When he had finished, Matthew crawled into bed, tired from the long and exciting night he had.

While Matthew was sleeping, the Lord Himself came to him in a dream and told him how very special the Baby Jesus was. He was the Son of God, born to save the world from their sins and give everlasting life to anyone who believed in Him. He was a baby King and the Lord told Matthew how his act of kindness and compassion meant so much to Him. His work of bringing the straw to fill the manger kept the Baby warm that night. Even though Matthew was a small creature, he gave of himself and did something REALLY BIG. Matthew woke up the next day and remembered his dream.

As he scurried to see the Baby in the manger, he smiled only as a mouse could do. When he saw the Baby King sleeping there, warm and safe, Matthew thanked God for sending this most precious Gift, His Son. "Thank you, Lord", Matthew said as he prepared for another busy night. He was happy when he came home to feed his family who were there waiting for him. He was happy to have been part of the most Special Night of all, the night our Lord Jesus was born.

As time went on, even after the Baby and his family had left, Matthew told everyone about the Special Night for as long as he lived. Telling the story filled him with happiness and joy. Even Matthew's children and grandchildren for generations went on to the tell the story that I am now telling you. No thing done for the Lord is ever too small when done from our heart.

The End

Try to find these words from the story about Matthew the Mouse:

ANGELS	MANGER
BABY	MOUSE
FAMILY	SHEPHERDS
GIFT	STABLE
INN	STAR
JESUS	STRAW

```
S M A N G E R F X E
T H R M E S O A O L
A P E S N R L M L B
R W U P W B N I A A
Q O D A H J S L N T
M S R O T E T Y G S
N T R F X S R L E H
S Q I A P U G D L G
B G N M Y S L O S T
A N N S Z R B A B Y
```

How much do you remember from the story about Matthew the Mouse? Answer these questions and find out! Circle the correct answer.

1   What kind of mouse was Matthew?

(a) deer (b) field (c) house

2   What kind of house did Matthew live in?

(a) stable (b) inn (c) forest

3   What was the loud noise that woke up Matthew?

(a) bird (b) baby (c) cow

4   What did the Baby use for a bed?

(a) crib (b) manger (c) basket

5   What was the bright light that scared Matthew?

(a) fire (b) star (c) lantern

6   Who did the angels visit in the field?

(a) shepherds (b) horses (c) lions

7   What did Matthew put in the manger to keep Baby Jesus warm?

(a) blanket (b) pillow (c) straw

EBUJML

JUMBLE

Look at the picture below and unscramble these words from the story about Matthew the Mouse.

GRAMNE   _____

BYBA   _____

WRSAT   _____

SUMEO   _____

```
S  M  A  N  G  E  R  F  X  E
T  H  R  M  E  S  O  A  O  L
A  P  E  S  N  R  L  M  L  B
R  W  U  P  W  B  N  I  A  A
Q  O  D  A  H  J  S  L  N  T
M  S  R  O  T  E  T  Y  G  S
N  T  R  F  X  S  R  L  E  H
S  Q  I  A  P  U  G  D  L  G
B  G  N  M  Y  S  L  O  S  T
A  N  N  S  Z  R  B  A  B  Y
```

Answers to quiz

1-field   2-stable
3-baby   4-manger
5-star   6-shepherds   7-straw

Answers to word jumble
MANGER, BABY, STRAW, MOUSE

The Mouse in the Manger as a children's play...

This story may be narrated as children act out the scenes, or you may take actual written parts of the story and have them memorize lines as a script. Try asking your children and (or) students how they might like to perform the story and if they have anything to add. You might be surprised with what they come up with. Children can be very imaginative and when given the opportunity to create, they will! There may be some side scenes and more than even YOU could have imagined to add to the story.

Characters:
Matthew the Mouse
Baby Jesus
Mary
Joseph
Shepherds
Angels
The Star?
Sheep
Other animals in the stable
Matthew's family

Scenes:
The stable
The field where the shepherds are
The inn (optional)

Music: (suggested traditional carols to be played or sung during the performance)
Away In A Manger
Silent Night
Hark the Herald Angels Sing
Angels We Have Heard On High
Go Tell It On The Mountain
Joy To The World
Mary's Little Boy Child
O Little Town of Bethlehem
What Child Is This

These are just a few...you may pick your favorites and add even more for fun!

Costuming and Props:
There is an almost limitless supply of both ideas and materials to be found around your own home, classroom, second hand stores, discount shops, the Internet and more. This part is the fun quest to find interesting items you can use and even re-use every year. Why not make it a holiday tradition?

Whether you are a parent or classroom teacher, the job you do is constant and sometimes thankless. So very much hard work goes into each day and each day is a new learning experience for our children and students. My wish is that this story has both touched and inspired you to keep up the hard work and be proud of the job you are doing!

Made in the USA
Columbia, SC
16 September 2024

42256936R00018